A Doubter's Prayer Book

by

William Cleary

Paulist Press

New York Mahwah

Library of Congress Cataloging-in-Publication Data

Cleary, William.
    A doubter's prayer book / by William Cleary.
        p.   cm.
    ISBN 0-8091-3454-3 (pbk.) :
    1. Faith—Prayer-books and devotions—
English.   I. Title.
  BV774.C57   1993
  242—dc20   93-40800
                                                 CIP

Published by Paulist Press
997 Macarthur Boulevard
Mahwah, New Jersey 07430

Printed and bound in the
United States of America

Dedication

To my everlasting brothers of the Society of Jesus
who taught me how to doubt

TABLE OF CONTENTS

A Doubter's First Prayer 1
Is Anyone There? 3
The Gift of Doubt 4
God of Magic? 8
Why Do You Pretend? 10
Too Much Doubt 14
Worthless Doubts 16
Are You Forgetting Me? 19
When Doubts Are Painful 22
I Am Full of Doubt 24
We Can't Understand 27
We Are Mystified 29
Barnyard Doubts 33
Are You a God of Love? 35
Fundamental Things 38
Are You There? 40
A Lifetime of Doubts 43
Life After Birth? 44
Spirit Stranger 47
Doubting Thomas 50
The Doubts of Jesus 51
The Symphony of Differences 56
Crabs Trust God 59
A Creed of Questions 60
A Doubting Apostles' Creed 65
A Doubter's Final Prayer 67

A Doubter's First Prayer

The first most puzzling part, dear God,
Is how to speak to you,
Great Spirit of the Universe,
Great Mystery I pursue.

You read me like an open book!
Your eyes are everywhere!
Are words required? I doubt they are—
But never doubt you're there . . .
    Or seldom doubt—that more the
      truth—
    (That never's premature),
    At times I even waffle on
    The few things that are sure.

I want to pray, I long to pray,
Will that work as a start?
So hear this prayer, All-Knowing God,
Or read it in my heart.

    I'm something like the man born blind
    That Christ gave some relief.
    I do believe though faith is weak:
    Help thou my unbelief.

1

How prone to doubt, how cautious are the wise.

HOMER

By doubting we come to the truth.

CICERO

Is Anyone There?

I stand outside and knock.
   Is anyone there?

If you did not like doubters, Loving Mystery,
   you could take away my doubts in a second:
      just appear to me in some undeniable way
      or speak to me as you supposedly spoke to the
         boy David
   and I will answer:
      Speak, Great Yahweh, for your servant is
         listening.
      I can hardly believe it's you.

But you choose not to do that . . .
   so I think you must like doubters.

So I stand at the door and knock.
   Anyone there?

The Gift of Doubt

I thank you, Holy Mystery, for the gift of doubt.
  I doubt if physical things are the way they seem.
  I doubt if spiritual things work the way we tend to
    think.
  I doubt if societal things are the way they should
    be.

I thank you for such doubts, Holy Wisdom, Holy Fire!

After all, do not religion and spirituality come from
      doubt?
  Death seems final, tragic. Sickness seems
      meaningless.
    Is there perhaps a deeper reality?
  Nature around us seems to have moods, and
      fearful power.
    Is there a Higher Power? A Spirit beyond moods?
  Powerful people are often cruelly selfish. The poor
      seem cursed.
    Is there a God of Justice?

Without the gift of doubting, I cannot begin to deal
      with these questions.

So, despite the pain of the uncertainty, I give thanks,
      dear God, for doubt
  for it draws me into my own best self

where I can know the presence of the Divine
    Mystery
    despite the uncertainty of its makeup or nature
    or limits or names,
where I can speak to a God
    without care for eloquence,
where I can join in the struggle for societal justice
    knowing only that God is, for once, on my side
    or, rather, that I am, this time, on God's side.

Give me many doubts, Great Giver of all that is good.

The man that feareth, Lord, to doubt
In that fear doubtest thee.

MACDONALD

Doubt is faith, in the main: but faith, on the whole,
is doubt.
We cannot believe by proof—but could we believe
without?

SWINBURNE

God of Magic?

Strange: the apparent absence of God
    is part of this world's design!
  Is it not an illusion?
    Like a magician's trick: the Divine seems to
        disappear!
  And is it not when we attempt to catch
    what the magician is doing
      that we find ourselves at prayer?

Prayer may often be an attempt
  to break through the fantasy
    that there may be no God.
Prayer may be just the attempt
  to live for awhile without the superstition
    that all that is . . . came about by accident,
    the horror that there is no one here with us,
  that we are alone after all,
  no ultimate meaning to anything,
    no discovery at the end of our search,
    no loss in choosing isolation, privilege, and
      despair.

Is not such a comforting atheism just a mirage,
  an optical phenomenon creating the illusion of
    refreshment
    with nothing there to quench our thirsting
      hearts?

But once atheistic, would I not still feel
   the invisible pull toward meaning
      which is your presence, Holy God?

Great Unknown Being, Intimate Spirit,
   you see my disbelief at your disappearance.
I know what happened, but I don't know how you
      did it.
Are you a God of magic or of mystery: which?

Why Do You Pretend?

God of Mystery,
  why is it you pretend not to exist?
  The chaos around us at times suggests
    a chaos in heaven instead of a creator in
      heaven.
Barbarous things are done
  by humans to each other,
  to thousands of them, millions of them
  over centuries—
  and we wonder: where is God?
Where are you?
How can it be that you are present at each and every
      violent scene
  and do nothing to protect the innocent?
Is that not almost the same thing as not existing?
At times there seems to be no God
  or only a God so preposterously powerless
  as to defy belief.
You don't seem to try to be plausible, God of Mystery!

How can a "God" be present at a grotesque injustice
      and not do anything?
Why is it you pretend not to be, O Holy Creator?
Is your ocean of mystery, perhaps
  far deeper than we had dreamed?
Can it be that you exist in an unknown
  far more vast than we have imagined?

Still, may your "way" be done.
That is easier for me to say than "your will be done"
since our word will is full of ambiguities
and suggests you cause everything
and thus leaves no room for evil

What you have created, the way reality is—in the
long run—
let that happen
I surrender to that, trusting you.
I can think of it as your "way," even if it is not your
will.
For how could you really will any unjust injury or
death,
thousands of which we witness daily in this world
of war and violence?
So I believe there is meaning in everything
even when I don't grasp what it is.
What remains for me, as for Job, is faith,
To keep faith,
Not to lose faith,
Not to give in to despair,
Not to curse the way the world is.
I look around at all you have made
and I know your strength, Holy Mystery,
your animals from ant to zebra
and almost a million species in between,
your earth and sky,

the spectacular mysteries of humankind, of mind,
of heart, of heroism.
Your marvels are beyond me.
I put my hand over my mouth.
Your way be done.

He that knows nothing, doubts nothing.

HERBERT

If you would be a real seeker after truth, it is necessary that at least once in your life you doubt, as far as possible, all things.

DESCARTES

Too Much Doubt

It is often only reasonable to doubt—
   so reason is often on doubt's side.
It seems the prayers of our human race go largely
            unanswered—
   so experience is largely on doubt's side.
Is not life only generous to us haphazardly
   and crushes us just as haphazardly?
   So this appears to be a haphazard world
     where ultimately everything is in doubt . . .

But no, Marvelous Creator, Creator of Marvels,
   not everything is in doubt.
   I cannot not believe you see me, hear me,
     know me within and without,
     and stand under somehow all that is
       though it obviously does not hang together
         as a God of Justice and Love would want.

Within you I live and move and have my being:
   that is the bedrock of my life,
   and there I begin to build a spirituality and a
         religion.
   There, for me, doubt ceases.
   It has done all the good it can.

Worthless Doubts

It's when the second hand is ticking around my
          watch
    and I am plodding from task to heavy task,
        just holding my world together so another hour
          can come about
    that I feel those futile doubts,
        those doubts I wish I did not have to have:
Is it worth it?
Am I achieving anything?
Is there hope after yesterday's tragedies?
Then I almost haven't energy to believe,
    no time for a vision or a hope or a prayer.

But it's when I'm touched with wonder
    that I can believe best.
It's when I see a courage and beauty that seems
          greater than human,
    that I see plain humanity but suspect inSpiration,
    when I hear a harmony among impossibly
          disparate sounds,
    when the grace of a story's events so take me by
          surprise
        that I cannot not pay attention.
It's when events like these revive a deep hope beneath
          my own despair
    that I begin to doubt my worthless doubts

to doubt if some doubting is really wise or
        justified,
and I may live for a moment in faith
and glimpse a faraway land of light
    as small as a star
        on the dark horizon of my inner world.

Question with reason even the existence of a God,
because, if there be one, he must more approve of the
homage of reason than that of blindfolded fear.

JEFFERSON

The person with humility will have acquired in the
last reaches of his beliefs the saving doubt of his own
certainties.

LIPPMANN

Are You Forgetting Me?

How long, Holy God, how long?
  Are you forgetting me?
  Could it be you hide your face from me?
How long must I feel this anguish,
  and live with sorrow all the day?
How long shall heart-sickness rule over me?
  (Our own way of the cross is not anything we
      planned.
  We walk on, step after step
    wondering: have we lost our way?
  Or could it be you want us where we are,
    and ask that we accept our precise tomorrow
      as it grows from today?)

Hear my prayer, dear God, and answer,
Give light to my eyes, my God, lest I sleep the sleep
    of death
  lest my enemies brag, "We have won the victory!"
  lest my foes take heart because I tremble.
  (Be with us, Holy Mystery, as life proceeds and
      crosses grow heavy.
  "Into Your hands I commend my spirit.")

But I shall have trusted your faithfulness,
  and my heart shall give thanks at your rescue.
Then I will sing my trustful song to you
  because you have been my God.

(God of every midnight and every sunrise,
be with us in our hopes,
be with us in our longing
to come to the light in your presence.)

after Psalm 13

When Doubts Are Painful

Save me, O God,
    for I am near drowning,
I sink in the quicksand
    where there is no foothold.
I have come into waters frightening and deep,
    and the waves sweep over me.

I am weary with despair,
    my throat is parched.
    my eyes grow dim with tears.
    More in number than the hairs of my head are
        my enemies.
    Those who would destroy me are mighty indeed.

Yet will I trust in you, O God, my God,
My times are in your hands for I am yours. . . .
                                    from Psalm 22

The first step toward philosophy is incredulity.

DIDEROT

Doubt is the beginning, not the end, of wisdom.

ILES

I Am Full of Doubt

Supposedly I stand before your holy face, O Greatest
     Mystery,
    knowing the warmth of your affection and care,
    hearing your voice in created things and in real
      events . . .
"Events": is not everything, stars, persons, books—
     an "event,"
    something happening,
    an "action" inasmuch as the creation of it is
     continuous
    and nothing has more substance or reality than
     that: an event?
Thus as Einstein explained, "Everything is
     essentially energy"
    not only because physicists hypothesize it best
     that way
    but also because philosophers experience it that
     way?

Questions explode on all sides, then implode with
     prior questions:
What am I to make of it all
    when you—who are most real—hide yourself,
and what seems so concrete and real
    —these walls, my companions nearby,
    my body-self—

are all illusion-packed, misleading guideposts,
     almost apparitions
("pseudo nonbeings" said a great philosopher—
     for they are all temporal, disintegrating,
        indefinable,
     as if they had no solid existence)?

So I am full of doubt again today.
     Am I able to know anything at all for certain?
     Am I who and where I feel I am?
        Or do I live in darkness, thinking it is light?
     What is happening around me right now?
        Is all this burgeoning mystery—you?
Ah! Do I have my being in the warmth of your love
        and care after all?

Doubt is the key to knowledge.

PERSIAN PROVERB

The most valuable human trait is the judicious sense
of what not to believe.

EURIPIDES

We Can't Understand

We praise you, Holy God, for our enemies,
  + for your steadfast love endures forever.
We praise you in all our defeats,
  + for heaven's care will have no end.
We praise you in our sorrows,
  + for your steadfast love endures forever.
And we praise you amidst our mourning,
  + for heaven's care will have no end.

  We can't understand the shadows around us
    or the never-ending victories of death and
      evil
        of pain and separation and failure
    or the betrayal of agreement and promise.
  But You stand at our side whatever befalls
    and we praise your mysterious presence—
      and absence.

Yes, we observe even your apparent absence . . .
  . . . for you seem to make no sound or
      movement
        that would tell us you are here.
We look for you, listen for you, in churches
      empty or full
    yet we are left with only our faith.

We praise you, Holy God, for our enemies,
+ for your steadfast love endures forever.
We praise you in all our defeats,
+ for heaven's care will have no end.
We praise you in our sorrows,
+ for your steadfast love endures forever.
And we praise you amidst our mourning,
+ for heaven's care will have no end.

We Are Mystified

Holy God, you have us mystified.
  You surround us with beautiful people whom we
        love almost infinitely,
  then you ask us to accept their mortality and
        fragility
  and often, ultimately, to accept their illnesses, their
        aging
    and finally their life's end—
  or sometimes their life's end long before their aging,
  and the death of their dearest dreams and greatest
        promise—
Why, Divine Creator? Why a world like this?

Holy God, we are mystified.
  Open our eyes to the gift of understanding
Granted, there is a balance to all this evil:
  the towering wonders of our world,
  the moments of ecstasy we have known—
  but why is the balance so often negative?
And many never discover enough of the bright side:
  how unspeakably beautiful are so many of our
        human race,
  how mysteriously dear certain individuals can
        become,
  how magnificent can be the natural blossoming of
        so many living things,

how spectacularly complex is the world beneath
        the microscope
how utterly splendid the sky and cosmos around us.

O unimaginable Creator of it all,
  you have us mystified.
  Open our hearts to the gift of understanding.
Why is this world the way it seems to be?
  A world that goes on almost as if you are absent
        almost as if you cannot hear our cries?
We want to ask: Can't Someone do something about
        this:
  this insanity, this injustice, this abuse?
  this appalling waste of desire, this pitiful defeat of
        promise?

But then someone observes a breath-taking sun
  setting over mountains blanketed in mist.
Someone discovers that the precious one they love
  loves them, wants to be with them,
Someone comes upon an ocean of caring within
        themselves,
  caring without limits or sandbars or shores,
Or someone is astounded by a fulfilled family tree
  bursting with intensity and fertility
  and human caring seemingly without limits;
        or any one of a thousand daily marvels

that can explode into our common human
consciousness,
And once again it seems that you are God
and You must exist
and be the heart and pinnacle of caring,
and be an ocean of colossal mystery,
and be infinitely and intimately present
even though out of reach of our comprehension.
Be so for us, Holy Mystery.
Visit us.
We know that is within your power. Amen.

There lives more faith in honest doubts . . . than in half the creeds.

TENNYSON

Doubting charms me not less than knowledge.

DANTE

Barnyard Doubts

The barnyard animals once hired
   an owl psychiatrist.
We're full of doubts about ourselves,
   they said. Can you assist?

Self-doubt had plagued the barnyard folk
   for years and years, of course,
Beginning when Cow felt despair
   when racing with the Horse.

But Horse felt shame about his role
   as gentlemanly stud,
And dreamed of flopping next to Pig
   beneath three feet of mud.

Poor Pig herself was found depressed,
   despairing in her moat
That she had failed so utterly
   to grow a beard like Goat.

And Goat would cluck and flap her hooves
   and peck and prance and sneeze
And try in vain to lay an egg
   which Chicken laid with ease.

The Chicken felt profound despair
   when Sheep would come in view,

For feathers were no help at all
   when winter breezes blew.

But Sheep felt ineffectual,
   would often want to scream
When she saw Cow producing milk,
   cheese, butter and ice cream.

Six animals all mystified
   why they had been created.
TO BE YOURSELF! wise Owl declared,
   so they went home—elated.

Are You a God of Love?

Sometimes I doubt that you are first a God of love.
Where did we get that idea?
Why is that always the first thing we tend
                to think of:
    God loves us?
That is crucial, of course.
    But that conviction ranks only second, or third.

What ranks first must be
    that you are a God of life and generosity
    and therefore of justice.
We give thanks, God of Justice,
    that there is enough here of the things we must
                have to live:
        so you expect us, justly, to share them.
                Of course.

Ah, but do we?
So—doubt about the God of Justice instantly arises:
    why does God not insist
        that the riches of this earth be shared?
Is it that to insist is not God's way?
Or is it that there is no God of Justice?

From this dilemma come three main religions:
    the religion of the rich:
        we have in heaven only a God of love;

the religion of the poor:
our God is a God of life and so of justice;
and the religion of the nonbelievers:
there obviously is no God.

At the heart of my reverence for you,
Mysterious Creating Spirit,
is my conviction
that above all it is justice you must love first
when so many suffer daily for the lack of it;
and thus you daily inspire people everywhere
to struggle for it
against the strong flowing current of financial
power,
political momentum and gender-based
oppression
I doubt completely that you endorse
the inequalities of the way things are
and the cruel impoverishment of the weak of the
earth.
I am full of doubts
that our overall manner of dealing with your gifts
(as if they did not all, in reality, come from you)
could be your preference.
Dear God of Justice—and also of Love,
I believe. Help thou my unbelief.

The more of doubt, the stronger faith.

BROWNING

When all beliefs are challenged together, the just and necessary ones have a chance to step forward and reestablish themselves.

SANTAYANA

Fundamental Things

The fundamentalists, I hear,
  build faith on solid rock,
The fundamental things of life
  are under key and lock.

Don't doubt! Don't give a second thought!
  To thinking call a halt.
Distrust yourself! You're full of sin,
  iniquity and fault.

Page one in the Koran is clear:
  "Don't ever doubt this book!"
(But if you're God and writing Truth,
  why fear a second look?)

The Bible too forbids some doubts:
  when Moses' credence stalled
And he struck that rock not once but twice,
  his passport was recalled.

Remember Zachariah? How
  to doubts he did succumb
When told his old wife was with child?
  He laughed. And got struck dumb.

But Jesus laughed at straining gnats
  and then great camels swallow

And mercilessly keeping rules
    that make one's prayers ring hollow.

So let us pray for wisdom's help
    to test which claims are just,
And live by fundamental things
    like justice, mercy, trust.

One final fundamental thing
    that every faith should prize
Is this: give all claims second thoughts—
    It takes time to be wise.

Are You There?

Look! I am before you exactly as I am . . .
   . . . and do you observe me as a loving parent
         would?
There is nothing I can hide,
   not even my doubts.
   It is with this doubting mind
      you have fashioned me, my God!
      Would you not be disappointed
         if I put the doubts aside when I come before
         you?
I have no doubt that I should be searching for you
   in all the roads and byways of my life
   in all my connections with other people,
      with children, with living things,
      with the earth and the cosmos.
And I do search for you, Elusive Being,
   perfect at hiding, perfect at silence,
   so perfect at seeming not to exist
      that bright people often disbelieve in you,
      or believe in a many-spirited divinity,
      or give up the search
      saying: "If there is a God, he must search for
         me, not I for him."

But does that question not make God unGodlike?
   For, first, God is not a he
      but necessarily genderless because bodyless,

and second, we do not know enough about God
   to know what God is likely to do,
and third, the so-called search for God
   seems a natural and constant decision of human
      beings
      through all of recorded history and before.

Yet where are you, Creating Spirit Beyond All
      Thought!
Will I always be unsure which direction to go in
      search of you?
Will I forever be wondering: can you hear my
      prayers—
   though you can have no hearing as I experience it?
And can you see my needs—
   though you can have no sight of the kind I know?
Have you space for me in your compassion—
   though you have no heart?

No doubt you do better than hear and see and feel
   but how you might do that escapes me utterly.
I am left with your presence—and my faith in that
      presence.
   Are you there?

Doubt is part of religion. All the religious thinkers were doubters.

SINGER

Modest doubt is . . . "the beacon of the wise."

SHAKESPEARE

A Lifetime of Doubts

Doubting's an elusive art
  that has to be instilled.
It doesn't start in infancy,
  it takes a mind quite skilled.

It comes at first with games and skits
  where dreaming is begun.
You're monstrous! or majestic!
  and doubt's part of the fun.

As life goes on, that sense of doubt,
  like sense of humor, grows.
It comes in moments of Aha!
  How given? No one knows.

Then doubts grow up—till they're mature,
  become a part of you,
Help separate what's dubious
  from what is surely true.

As we grow old our doubts age too,
  become familiar friends.
With final gifts—of vision—
  all the need for doubting ends.

Life After Birth?

Once upon a time, twin submicroscopic zygotes were conceived in the same womb, bursting with twin possibilities. Side by side they blossomed, multiplying cells geometrically, swimming about in a rich and delicious sea that was their world.

Embryos they soon became, and pleasure coursed through all their parts. They stretched and flipped and wriggled about through many mysterious ups and downs, each of their multitudinous cells changing and complexifying as it doubled and doubled and doubled again.

As their months of swimming finally numbered six, they each began to hear sounds of what seemed like the whole world humming, then the humming became song-like, and finally they could hear strange gusts of sound.

"Who's there?" asked one, vibrating.

"It's just me," said the other.

"What's that hum?" asked the one. "Are you making that hum?"

"Not me," said the other. "I'm diving around here in perfect silence. Whee!"

Suddenly they crashed together and wrinkled up their faces in pain.

"Why such pain?" asked the one. "Do you think we should try to figure out the pain we feel and sounds we hear?"

"Let's do that," answered the other.

So they began to put their heads together on a regular basis. But they could not arrive at any conclusions. Other mysteries popped up in the conversation. What were these arms and legs all about, not at all perfect for swimming. They felt their faces: what was this nose for, these teeth buds, these two closed sockets atop their faces.

"It's deeply mysterious," said the one.

"Absurd," said the other.

"Wait," said the one. "I would not say absurd. That would not harmonize with what I already know. In fact, I feel strangely loved by the warm world around me. Surely there's some kind of mother who will explain it all someday."

"Dream on," said the other.

But one day the world, instead of growing larger, began to contract a little, grow smaller.

"What was that?" asked the one.

"A quake!" cried the other. "We are about to die!"

"I can't believe that," said the one, trying to be calm. "This world is too wonderful to end up in tragedy."

Then came another squeeze.

"Something new is about to happen," said the one. "Perhaps we are going to be born into another world, a larger world."

"Or just be squeezed to death," answered the other.

But the one said: *"Mother would not do that to us: WOULD YOU, MOTHER?"* The shout echoed throughout the world but brought no reply.

"You see, there is no mother," said the other.

The one kept silent a while. Then, though trembling with dread, she spoke hopefully: *"How could there be meaning in some parts of life if there were not meaning beneath it? Life thus far has often been joyful and meaningful, despite the mysteries of our useless faces and the muffled sounds around us and the pain we feel when we crash together. So I for one can't believe we will be squeezed to death."*

And the one was right. They were not squeezed to death but squeezed to life, where they discovered all those things their eyes had not seen, nor had their ears heard, nor had it entered into their hearts to dream of.

46

Spirit Stranger

Spirit Stranger, are you with us
In this room? Now, really here?
Do you know our names and faces,
All our graces, all our fear?
   Spirit Stranger, do you know me?
   Do you recognize this voice?
   Are my gifts and limitations
   Your creations? Your good choice?
      Why, Dear Stranger, must you be
      So invisible to Me?
      And so silent, without sound
      Warning me that you're around?
Spirit Mystery, can it be
You are looking straight at me?
Though it be naive to do
I pray someday to look at you.

Spirit Stranger! It's beyond me
How you could be really there
And be reading all my feelings!
If you do, what good is prayer?
   What's the use of song and worship
   If you "know it all" before?
   We are taught to sing you praise,
   But wouldn't Silence praise you more?
      And, dear Stranger, I'm afraid
      I'm not anything you made.

How could you, who made our sky,
Waste your time on such as I?
See how potters mold their clay,
Washing every flaw away?
I'm so flawed, dear potter-god!
Ah, your taste in pots is odd!

Spirit, may we call you Mother?
Father? Brother? Sister? Friend?
Names all fail, you're wrapped in mystery,
Things we'll never comprehend.
  So today I'll call you "stranger,"
  Little knowing what I mean:
  Someone close and yet unreachable,
  Or somewhere in between.
    Spirit Stranger, this, to me
    Is your strangest mystery:
    How our sorrows you can bear
    And not die in your despair!

Spirit Stranger, grant that we
Not forever strangers be.
May there come that morning when
We shall see your Face. Amen.

All uncertainty is fruitful . . . so long as it is accompanied by the wish to understand.

MACHADO

Religion isn't yours firsthand until you doubt it right down to the ground.

SAYRE

Doubting Thomas

We love you, Thomas.
In John 20 you comfort us.
You were at first so excited by the prophetic Jesus
    that you confused him with the gospel he brought.
But he died
    and you felt so deceived!
You had believed so thoroughly
You would not be deceived again, so you had to
            touch the wounds
    to believe he had actually died but also had
            conquered death.
Then did you understand?
    Ah, it was his gospel that was immortal,
        that the Anawim and the insignificant are blest,
        that the God of Justice will prevail,
        that there is hope even when hope is gone,
        that God loves the world despite all
            appearances!

You teach us, Thomas,
    that one thing is beyond doubt:
    unless we feel the mark of the nails, we shall not
            discover God,
    unless we care about the wounded, the divine shall
            elude us.
That's Matthew 25. That's Isaiah 58. Is that not John
        20?

The Doubts of Jesus

As a youngster, what might have been his doubts? Perhaps some of these?

Is my mother not a little strident, with all her talk of routing the proud in the imagination of their hearts, putting down princes from their thrones, and sending the rich away empty? Isn't that a little strong?

My father, content to be a carpenter: has he really heard the voices of angels? Was it not his imagination working overtime? He's had no rabbi's training.

Who are these Romans? How can they abuse us without being struck dead by Yahweh?

As a twelve year old, *what were those questions Jesus was asking the scribes, the time he was separated from his parents? Could it have been doubt that set his mind ablaze, blotting out even a thought he might be lost from family or clan?*

The Nameless One, where is he, masters? Why do we not see him?

If he created light, why does he dwell in darkness now?

Can God live in a scripture? a temple? or museum?

Can children speak to God, and can you teach me how?

Does God love helpless children? Does God bless the poor and lowly?

Or are the rich and powerful the most divinely blest?
And when Messiah comes, will he be young? Will he
seem holy?
Or will he be a poor man like the prophet Micah
guessed?
His "Good News for the poor!" Will that be bad news
for the wealthy?
Will he push princes from their thrones as Amos has
foresaid?
He brings sight to the blind! Does that mean blindness
for the healthy?
And will he be a he or could he be a she instead?

As an adolescent, there in his Nazareth synagogue,
could he believe what he heard in the Prophets and the
Psalms?

In Jeremiah: God is a "God of justice" whose heart is
"set on justice"?
In Psalm 99: "Yahweh loves justice"? How can that be,
with so much injustice around?
In Isaiah: "I, Yahweh, have called you to serve the
cause of justice." Called us? Called me?
In Amos, Hosea, Micah: one decisive theme—justice?
In Deuteronomy: "Justice, and justice alone, you shall
pursue." Alone?
Could it all be true? Is this the Voice of God?

Leaving home, *did he not have his hesitations? Was his mind so clear that he never questioned what was supposedly God's teaching?*

Do my oppressed countrymen really seem like a chosen people, God's own nation? Do they in fact really have the wit and courage to be a light to all the nations on the earth, as Genesis has demanded?

Will anyone be interested in what I have been preaching in my dreams?

What might be the price I'll have to pay for saying the last shall be first? Men who say such things have died on the cross for it: shall I come to that?

As he chose his Twelve, *were they really as promising as he needed them to be?*

This rock of a man: will he ever be anything but a fishy-smelling loud mouth?

Poor John: will he and his brother James be able to stand up to the others? Will these gentle "Sons of Thunder" (Ha!) even survive?

Will Thomas ever get beyond his doubting?

Will soft-talking Philip ever stop romanticizing?

Will the enthusiasm of dear Judas hold up through the rough times? He will hold us together all right, but will his expertise be enough?

When his popularity was at its highest, *was Jesus at all doubtful about what to do and what to say?*

Am I getting through? Is anything happening? These stories I think up: are people figuring them out at all? Or am I oversimplifying what is naturally complex? Are my enemies all that wrong? Is this spirit that's got hold of me God's—or Satan's?

As some people turned against him, *did he not stop to question what he was doing?*

Can it be wise to tell the people what they do not want to hear?
How can I ask the radicals, so justly angry, not to live by the sword?
Am I not a coward, to take no vengeance for the murder of my cousin John? Does appeasement not encourage arrogance?

Stumbling in agony along the way of the Cross, *did he not harbor bitter thoughts?*

Peter! James! John! Could you not wait up one hour with me?
Friend, do you betray me with a kiss?
They all have fled.
My God, my God, why have <u>you</u> forsaken me?

I respect faith but doubt is what gets you an education.

MIZNER

A faith which does not doubt is dead faith.

UNAMUNO

The Symphony of Differences

The orchestra was tuning up
In a concert hall shaped like a cup.
The seats were filling up to hear
The first performance of the year.

"Tubas are thick," remarked the Flute,
Tooting soft in Oboe's ear,
"And make disgusting sounds to boot,"
Oboe replied. (No one could hear.)

"This isn't a religious sound,"
Said Flute, grimacing all around
While trumpets whined,
    and bagpipes bleat
In pandemonium complete.

The Oboe wrinkled up her face:
"Those flugelhorns are a disgrace,
And cymbals are a crashing bore,
I just can't take them anymore."

Flute whispered, "Chimes believe in
        God!
I find their clangs extremely odd.
And bugles honk out graceless sounds
Like wild, unbalanced merry-go-
        rounds."

The Oboe scowled: "Strings are uptight
With guilt and dread all
   through the night."
And Flute said condescendingly:
"Only woodwinds can set you free!"

Piano plunged down low, then high,
A sax was screaming at the sky,
The trombones blared belief in dreams
While Piccolo soared to extremes.
One English horn went sharp—whereat
The zither shrieked the world was flat.

While double basses plunked off-key
And brass would blast disgustingly,
Violas soon, like wounded gulls,
Were begging God for miracles;
And Cellos wailed about their grief,
While Snare Drum sneered his disbelief.

Then slowly one rich chord was born
First small and tortured, sad, forlorn,
Then grew in scope and then broke free,
A marvel of diversity,
Splaying bright, hopeful melodies

Atop rich, longing harmonies,
All girded up with chords afire
From burning depths of deep desire,
Expressing wildly diverse themes
And mysteries beyond its dreams.

Oboe and Flute saw they'd been wrong
To think "tune up" could be a song,
And learned, but for diversity,
No heart could dream of harmony.

Crabs Trust God

Crabs long ago decided crabs must
God trust, God trust,
Round their world they bump and blunder
backwards (backwards!)
while above, around and under
the tide's unfathomable green seethings
sway and swerve them, and they see things
backwards:
watching the past fade into the pattern,
helpless to foresee, forelearn,
foretell, anticipate or surmise
life's next inevitable surprise.
Crabs long ago decided
crabs must
God trust.

A Creed of Questions

I love to ask: Is that God real
   Whom ancients have adored?
Is there as well a Jesus Christ
   God's only son, our Lord?

I love to ask: Was he conceived
   Through Spirit's ebbs and flows,
Born of a virgin, suffered, died
   And on the third day rose?

I love to ask: Did he ascend
   And sit at God's right hand
From whence he'll come to some wide plain
   Where dead and living stand?

I love to ask: What of the Spirit,
   What of the Church, his Wife,
The circle of saints, the forgiveness of sins,
   And everlasting life?

There's faith in all this questioning,
   And harmony for all,
But answering creates two sides,
   Divided by a wall.

So I ask if Apostles' Creeds
  Aren't less worthwhile than be
Apostles' questions, fears, and doubts—
  And solidarity?

To believe with certainty we must begin with doubting.

STANISLAUS

An honest person can never surrender an honest doubt.

MALONE

Faith and doubt are the twin offspring of mystery.

MATTUCK

Doubts make us wise.

UCEDA

A Doubting Apostles' Creed

I BELIEVE IN YOU, Mysterious God, our parent and
*   our love,*
* creator of sky and earth,*
AND IN YOU, JESUS THE CHRIST, God's messenger,
*   our prophet,*
* who was conceived as a Light to the World,*
* born of a revolutionary woman,*
* suffered under a violent military regime*
*   for your solidarity with the oppressed;*
* and was, against God's will, crucified, died and*
*   was buried.*
YOU DESCENDED INTO DEATH,
* and the third day*
*   were again somehow present to your disciples,*
YOU ASCENDED INTO LIFE,
* and abide now in the presence of God and in our*
*   presence,*
AND FROM THENCE YOU COME DAILY in the needy
* to judge the living and the dead.*

I BELIEVE IN YOU, HOLY SPIRIT,
* in a catholic and borderless world,*
* in the communion of saints of every religion,*
* in the forgiveness of sins, as we forgive others,*
* and in resurrection to come after death*
*   to a life everlasting and merry, Amen.*

Doubt is not below knowledge but above it.

ALAIN

Doubt is the vestibule which all must pass before they can enter into the temple of truth.

COLTON

I believe in the sun
  even when it is not shining.
I believe in love
  even when I do not feel it.
I believe in God
  even when he is silent.

JEWS IN GERMANY 1939 (anonymous)

A Doubter's Final Prayer

O God, your eyes have searched my soul,
You've known me utterly,
You know when I sit down and when I rise,
You know the roads I walk along,
You know where I lie down,
You know my fond delusions and disguise.
> Before my thought becomes a word, You know
> what I will say,
> You know my past, my present, and my plans,
You lay a kind and loving hand of comfort on my
> head,
You hold me, with the cosmos, in your hands.

Where might I go to hide from you,
My Lover and my God?
If I ascend the heavens, you are there.
You'd find me in the house of death,
You'd find me in the dawn,
Or far at sea—you'd find me anywhere.
> If I should say, "I'll hide myself in darkness
> and in night,"
> The darkest night is bright as day to you,
To you I turn my human face and know that you
> are there,
Your presence almost too good to be true.

—Psalm 139